This book is for

_____

May you lose your unnecessary burdens
And gain a richer, freer life.

_____

[DATE]

WHAT HAVE
YOU
GOT TO LOSE?

EXPERIENCE A RICHER LIFE
BY LETTING GO OF THE THINGS THAT
CONFUSE, CLUTTER AND CONTAMINATE

BY STEPHEN ARTERBURN

THOMAS NELSON PUBLISHERS
Since 1798

www.thomasnelson.com

Nashville Dallas Mexico City Rio De Janeiro Beijing

Published in Nashville, TN, by Thomas Nelson. Thomas Nelson is a trademark of Thomas Nelson, Inc.

Thomas Nelson, Inc., titles may be purchased in bulk for educational, business, fundraising, or sales promotional use. For information, please email SpecialMarkets@ThomasNelson.com.

Unless otherwise noted, all scripture references are from the *New King James Version of the Bible* (NKJV) ©1979, 1980, 1982, 1992, Thomas Nelson, Inc., Publisher. Other scriptures come from the following: *New Century Version®* (NCV). Copyright © 1987, 1988, 1991 by Thomas Nelson, Inc. All rights reserved. *The King James Version of the Bible* (KJV). *The New International Version of the Bible* (NIV) © 1984 by the International Bible Society. Used by permission of Zondervan Bible Publishers. *The Living Bible* (TLB) ©1971 by Tyndale House Publishers, Wheaton, IL. Used by permission. *The Message* (MSG) © 1993. Used by permission of NavPress Publishing Group. *The Holy Bible, New Living Translation* (NLT) © 1996. Used by permission of Tyndale House Publishers, Inc., Wheaton, Ill. All rights reserved.

Cover and Interior Design by Visibility Creative.

ISBN-10: 1-4041-0492-5

ISBN-13: 978-14041-0492-1

Printed in the United States of America.

INTRODUCTION

This book is about a miracle that you can experience. No, it's not a wonder drug or a foolproof diet plan. It's the miracle of addition through subtraction. Huh? No, really. Less can be so much more, especially when you're trying to eliminate unnecessary burdens from your life. Want to lose weight? Eat less. Want to improve your finances? Spend less. Want to reduce stress and simplify your life? Read this book.

For more than twenty years I've led counseling ministries to help men and women take life–changing actions to improve their lives. In *What Have You Got to Lose?* I'm offering biblical concepts to guide you through seven steps for relieving yourself of baggage and living more abundantly. As you journey through this book you'll become better equipped to lose the unnecessary burdens that confuse, clutter, and contaminate your life.

If you've wanted to change something in your life, this book is for you. It's simple, practical advice that will help you through any positive life change—whether you're trying to improve your health, enrich your relationships, or even just feel better about yourself. Change is tough, but these steps can help you resolve the issues that hold you back from accomplishing your goals. You're not in this alone. Give it a try. After all, what have you got to lose?

SEVEN KEYS TO
LOSING YOUR BURDENS

Surrender. "So humble yourselves under the mighty power of God, and at the right time he will lift you up in honor" (1 Peter 5:6 NLT). You must be willing to discover what is driving your negative behaviors and want healing more than you want your false comforts. You are able to accomplish your goals and surrender to His way of doing things.

Acceptance. "O LORD, you have examined my heart and know everything about me" (Psalm 139:1 NLT). You must be determined to face and own the emotional issues, pain, and loss that you uncover behind your emotional burdens. Accept the reality of your situation and your need for help. Stay in the reality of your life. God sees your heart. He knows your need and will provide the help you require.

Confession. "Confess your sins to each other and pray for each other so that you may be healed" (James 5:16 NIV). Come out of hiding. Open up to God and others about the reality of your struggles. While it is often difficult to admit your shortcomings and areas of weakness, it is what keeps us honest and real with each other. Confession truly is good for the soul. You must find people you can trust who can handle your secrets and help you heal.

Responsibility. "For we are each responsible for our own conduct" (Galatians 6:5 NLT). Taking responsibility for change, moving out of the victim position, and owning up to your mistakes are necessary to losing your burdens. When you are hurt or experience loss, it's easy to blame others or feel like a victim. However, you must believe that God will bring purpose and meaning out of pain, and then you must move on.

Forgiveness. "If you forgive those who sin against you, your heavenly Father will forgive you" (Matthew 6:14 NLT). Forgive your own failures and the failures of those who have hurt you. Forgiveness is not optional in the Christian life and yet many of us hold on to bitterness and wonder why we don't experience joy and other benefits of the Christian life. When you give up grudges and make restitution for past wrongs, you experience spiritual blessings.

Transformation. "All praise to God, the Father of our Lord Jesus Christ. God is our merciful Father and the source of all comfort. He comforts us in all our troubles so that we can comfort others. When they are troubled, we will be able to give them the same comfort God has given us" (2 Corinthians 1:3–4 NLT). Transform your struggle, pain, and loss into a purposeful mission. God's way is to take those things you have suffered and use them for His glory. Out of pain and difficulty come compassion for others and a willingness to reach out because of the grace and mercy shown to you.

Preservation. "So make every effort to apply the benefits of these promises to your life. Then your faith will produce a life of moral excellence. A life of moral excellence leads to knowing God better" (2 Peter 1:5). Perseverance is required to make it through life's inevitable struggles and keep the spiritual gains made. When you understand the signs and phases of relapse, you will learn to maintain your victories.

*Come to Me, all you who labor and are heavy laden,
and I will give you rest. Take My yoke upon you and learn from Me,
for I am gentle and lowly in heart, and you will find rest for your souls.
For My yoke is easy and My burden is light.*

Matthew 11:28-30

LOSE THE BURDEN OF CONTROL ... GAIN THE FREEDOM OF SURRENDER

When He had called the people to Himself, with His disciples also,
He said to them, "Whoever desires to come after Me,
let him deny himself, and take up his cross, and follow Me.
For whoever desires to save his life will lose it,
but whoever loses his life for My sake and the gospel's will save it."

Mark 8:34–35

L ife is difficult. Just when we think we have things under
control, something happens to remind us that control
is elusive. The children who brought such pleasure early on
now bring headaches and heartbreaks with rebellion and even
rejection. The promotion at work gives us more money but robs
us of valuable time and peace of mind. The truth is, we aren't

really in control. And until we come to terms with this reality, our lives are destined to be full of anxiety, fear of the future, guilt over the past, and anger at others.

We can, however, pretend to be in control, and many of us do this. We pretend by lying to ourselves about the quick fix that fixes nothing or the instant solution that only makes matters worse. We delude ourselves with the mantras of all those who have failed before us:

✳ All I have to do is have more willpower.

✳ All I have to do is quit being so lazy and do more.

✳ All I have to do is take more control of my life.

✳ I can do anything if I try hard enough.

Then, when we no longer believe the lie that we can do whatever we set our minds to, we succumb to the opposite extreme, believing we can do nothing and all is hopeless.

Rather than fight with the same ineffective weapons that have backfired so many times, why not surrender this battle? Pull out the white flag and vigorously wave it. Give yourself over to a higher authority; relinquish control to God. He can be trusted, especially when you feel weak and defeated. As the apostle Paul said, "When I am weak, then I am strong" (2 Corinthians 12:10). When you come to the end of yourself, God is waiting to step in and provide rest for the weary, and chances are you could use a little reprieve from this exhausting fight. After all, what have you got to lose?

Why not give up the illusion of control and yield to God's mercy and grace? Peter said, "Be humble under God's powerful hand so he will lift you up when the right time comes" (1 Peter 5:6 NCV). Acknowledge your weakness and invite God into the process. Accept the radical notion that if you could have fixed your problems on your own, under your own power, you would have done so by now and the struggles would be over. You have to make an admission. You have to admit that you cannot handle life on your own. You have to admit that God can. And you have to let Him do this work, even if it means working with God's people to accomplish the transformation that is necessary. When you let go of your life and put it into God's hands, you are in good hands.

God is the Creator of all life and the Lord of the universe. But since the Garden of Eden, men and women have continually played God and tried unsuccessfully to rule over their own destinies. From Genesis through Revelation, Scripture reveals humankind's natural incapacity to live healthy, God-pleasing lives. The Old Testament describes a colorful assortment of characters who turned their backs on God's ways and inevitably experienced fear, foolishness, and failure. Yet some of them surrendered to the ultimate power of God, allowing Him to intervene in their lives with divine power and wisdom. In the New Testament, Christ's death on the cross made God's intervention even more accessible—He took upon Himself the willfulness and rebellion of the entire world. His resurrection brought hope for new life.

The road of self-effort and control has not taken you where you wanted to go. Proverbs 14:12 warns, "Before every man there lies a wide and pleasant road that seems right but ends in death" (TLB). To stay on this road is to choose further heartache and destruction. Consequently, we must be willing to admit that our lives have spun out of control. Self-control and our forms of self-treatment have failed us and must be abandoned.

Although we are limited by our weaknesses, God is not. By acknowledging that He alone has the power to change the course of our lives, we surrender to Him our powerlessness and begin the process of spiritual renewal. Only when we relinquish our control to God does He release His supernatural power in our lives, and it is only through His power that we can be transformed by the renewing of our minds (Romans 12:2).

Every limitation we have can be seen as an invitation from God to do for us what we cannot do for ourselves. When we surrender, we don't just give up or play dead or wait for God to fix us. Instead, we become active participants with God in making a new path of hope toward healing. We drop our guard and give up our solitary and isolated efforts to heal. We sincerely and humbly reach out to others who can help us restore our lives to spiritual vitality. Surrender is not passivity, nor is it resignation. Its motion requires an active and conscious turning toward God wherein we reflect our willingness to submit to His power by living out our newfound truth and sharing it with others.

Surrender means:

✳ humbling ourselves before the God of the universe.

✳ admitting that God is all powerful and releasing our struggles to Him.

✳ refusing to escape into the old patterns, habits, and attitudes that continue to distract us, and add to the destruction of our lives.

✳ no longer saying, "I can handle this myself."

✳ submitting to God's way of doing things even when we don't understand.

✳ getting past our pain and fear and clinging to our hope in God and His love for us.

✳ setting aside our human understanding, becoming childlike, and acknowledging we have no answers that work.

Surrender allows us to grow as we submit to God's authority. In order to submit, we must trust that God has good things for us and that His plans and purposes far outweigh what we bring to the table.

The difference between surrender and control looks like this:

SURRENDER	CONTROL
God is the Master of the universe.	I can master all things.
God's perspective is higher than mine.	What I feel is all that is important.
My circumstances are part of God's eternal perspective.	If God is God, my circumstances must be changed now.
I must allow God's plans to open up before me.	My plans are all that matter. I demand immediate results.
I am not alone and never will be.	If there is a God, He is not part of my life and I alone can change my reality.
I accept life knowing that all things will work together for my good.	I blame God when life doesn't go the way I think it should.

SURRENDER

It is never too late to abandon yourself to God's power and authority. He can redeem lost time and work His purposes in your life. And when you release yourself from self–effort and striving, a huge burden is lifted.

If you can grasp this concept of surrender and implement it, you can be free from your obsessions and find a new life you never dreamed could be so great. But before you can have that life, you must surrender the one you have.

Surrender acknowledges God's existence and is the first act of faith that will begin your transformation. Acknowledge that He is in the driver's seat and you are along for the ride. Your way hasn't worked and His grace is sufficient. His power will be made perfect in your weakness. Surrender leads to healing and the promise God gave us in Jeremiah 29:14: "'I will let you find me,' says the LORD. 'And I will bring you back from your captivity'" (NCV).

Once the decision to surrender all to Christ is made, transformation begins.

LOSE THE DO-IT-YOURSELF MENTALITY . . . GAIN THE GIFT OF GRACE

You have been saved by grace through believing.
You did not save yourselves; it was a gift from God.

Ephesians 2:8 NCV

Grace is divine, a gift from God to you. He offers new life based on nothing you have to offer. There is no way to earn His affections or coax His love for you. He already delights in you and befriends you. When you fail, He says, "Not to worry. I am with you and we can start afresh. Lean on Me, not on your own strength. I am strong when you are weak. I have a plan and purpose for your life that I'm dying to reveal."

Grace seems too good to be true, but it's authentic. There is no pretending. The God of all grace is compassionate. He cares deeply, and He has the capacity to be intimately involved in our lives. His friendship and promises are mind–boggling. By grace, God has the astounding ability to see sin, not excuse it, but love anyway. He hangs out with the failed, the most desperate, and the most defeated. He walks along, holding our hands, and pours out healing salve, mercy, and hope.

Grace teaches us: "With My help, you can keep moving toward the goal. However, remind yourself about Me. I'm going to be here every day. Without Me, your heart will condemn you. But I won't withhold any good thing from you if you walk uprightly."

The grace of God is revealed through the divine person and work of Jesus Christ. He both embodied grace and benefited from God's grace. By His death and resurrection on the cross, Christ brought salvation to each of us and restored our broken relationship with God. The Holy Spirit, called the Spirit of grace (Hebrews 10:29), is the one who binds Christ to us so we can receive forgiveness, adoption, and new life.

Grace requires faith. We must trust in the mercy of God and realize His favor on us even though it is undeserved. This unmerited favor is a free gift given by our affectionate heavenly Father. We must remember that God's grace abounds in our lives. He is for us, not against us. He cheers us on to victory, and He uses others to pour out that grace in our lives as well.

If you find you are beating yourself up all the time, saying to yourself things you would never say to someone else, then you have Grace Deficiency. If you think you are so bad no one can love you, you have GD. If you judge yourself based solely on your appearance or your accomplishments, you have GD. Thankfully, this misery–inducing disease has a cure! God's extravagant grace is what heals it. Give yourself a grace transfusion through reading God's Word, communing with His people, and utilizing a new vocabulary for your self–talk. It is time you started treating yourself the way God treats you . . . with grace!

SURRENDER

LOSE THE UNREALISTIC EXPECTATIONS . . . GAIN REAL HOPE

Lead me by your truth and teach me,
for you are the God who saves me.
All day long I put my hope in you.

Psalm 25:5 NLT

One problem many people have with Christianity is that they are offered some false promises if they ever surrender their lives to Jesus. They are told that everything changes and happiness is the result, but this is simply not true. Becoming a Christian does not mean everything will immediately change. Real–life residue is present that must be processed out of our lives. And some realities like loss, struggle, temptation, and betrayal cause us to be anything but happy.

Reevaluating our expectations is both necessary and an important part of accepting reality. Here are some common, unrealistic expectations to reconsider:

1. I must be perfect for God to work in me. Holding this thought, we tend to cover up problems and be dishonest about our struggles because we think God is looking for perfection in order to work. But the reality is that He invites us to be His with every wrinkle and flaw. One of the problems of the modern church is that we are often taught to cognitively fix things by declaring a scripture like John 8:32, "Then you will know the truth, and the truth will make you free" (NCV). This scripture is absolutely right on! But we need to read the one before it as well (v. 31): "Jesus said to the Jews who believed in him, 'If you continue to obey my teaching, you are truly my followers.'"

Jesus is telling us that the truth cannot just be read, but must be lived out in our lives—following His commands, loving one another, seeing ourselves as He says we are, picking up our daily cross and following Him, crucifying the flesh, etc. Do you see a difference?

The Living Truth says no to self and selfish desires and requires an authentic life lived with others and before the

Lord. The truth transforms us, but we have to cooperate during the process in order to look like the Christ who does the transforming. Sadly, we see little of this transformation in our churches because the church often penalizes us for being honest. Problems are hidden as we are encouraged to hang on to Jesus and put on a happy face.

God didn't hide truth in His Word. Throughout the Bible there are unflattering details of sins committed by biblical characters, and yet God so loved the world that He gave His only begotten Son (John 3:16). This is powerful. God sees our imperfections and is able to transform us anyway! But we have to let Him do His work!

2. I've screwed up so many times it's just too late. It's never too late with God. Repeat this twenty times until it sinks into your thick skull! God doesn't hold grudges and He certainly doesn't keep on punishing you for sins already confessed. He forgives and calls you to Him. When you accept guilt and shame from your past, you basically tell God that His sacrifice didn't matter. Jesus Christ has taken all your guilt and shame to the cross and doesn't want you holding on to it. He says, "I'll take your failures and build your future." And He has a great future planned for you. Witness the life of the apostle Peter and his track record of failures and victories. That's our God—using our failures and redeeming our losses. But we've got to be honest and not hide our faults and struggles.

3. I can do this alone. Perhaps this is the mother of all unrealistic expectations. If you could do it alone you would have done it by now. Going it alone feeds your destructive appetites. God uses connections to heal us. Going it alone is just a very long and painful path to going right back to where you were before.

When you surrender your unrealistic expectations about how God does or doesn't work in your life, you open yourself to receive the real hope He offers.

I do not mean that I am already as God wants me to be. I have not yet reached that goal, but I continue trying to reach it and to make it mine. Christ wants me to do that, which is the reason he made me his. Brothers and sisters, I know that I have not yet reached that goal, but there is one thing I always do. Forgetting the past and straining toward what is ahead, I keep trying to reach the goal and get the prize for which God called me through Christ to the life above.

Philippians 3:12—14 NCV

SURRENDER

LOSE THE LIES OF THE PAST ... GAIN TRUE PERSPECTIVE ON LIFE

O Lord, you have examined my heart and know everything about me.

Psalm 139:1 NLT

Change, even when desired and positive, can be stressful. When contemplating change, one important question to ask yourself is this: "Will I be confronted with issues in my life I have worked so hard to avoid?"

If you accept the challenge to change your life, you will have to face moments of pain from the past you might prefer be left alone, deal with relationship difficulties, and make changes in possibly all aspects of your lifestyle and habits. Change is possible. One step at a time, through making decisions and evaluating your needs, you will find the answers you need.

ACCEPTANCE

Once you fully surrender the battle for change to God, you must open your eyes to reality and stop lying to yourself or making excuses. This is a vital step in the process. Incredible insight concerning truth is offered by Fyodor Dostoevsky in his novel *The Brothers Karamazov.*

> The important thing is to stop lying to yourself. A man who lies to himself, and believes his lies, becomes unable to recognize the truth, either in himself or anyone else, and he ends up losing respect for himself as well as others. When he has no respect for anyone, he can no longer love and, in order to divert himself, having no love in him, he yields to his impulses. Indulges in the lowest forms of pleasure, and behaves in the end like an animal, in satisfying his vices. And it all comes from lying—lying to others and to yourself.

You have to face reality or you end up lying to yourself and others. Tough questions must be asked and answered:

* ✳ What is my part in causing this problem?

* ✳ How do I usually respond to difficulty?

* ✳ What unmet needs do I have that I try to meet through this bad habit?

ACCEPTANCE

✳   Am I hung up on why my life feels so out of control?

✳   Am I disconnected from others?

✳   Do I live in denial, refusing to acknowledge my problem and the impact it has on my life?

The words of Jesus in John 16:33 provide truth and hope. Jesus tells His disciples, "These things I have spoken to you, that in Me you may have peace. In the world you will have tribulation; but be of good cheer, I have overcome the world."

Jesus doesn't lie to us. As the Son of God, He is incapable of lying. He tells us that difficulty and suffering will be part of life— He wants us to know reality. And this is the reason we can trust Christ: He is the Truth and He speaks truth. Jesus offers hope. He has overcome the world! "I am the way, the truth, and the life. No one comes to the Father except through Me," He declares (John 14:6). "And you shall know the truth, and the truth shall make you free" (John 8:32). Acceptance involves first realizing the full depth of your problem, which means seeing life as it really is.

Often it is easier to replace these realities with lies of our own making. We tell ourselves there really is nothing we can do, that it isn't our fault we got into this mess. Or we fear that to face the reality will mean facing pain, which is potentially worse than letting our problem continue and merely surviving through life. Or we assume that if God wanted to, He would take this burden from us. He would take away this pain if it were His will.

All are very tempting lies to grasp, but when we reach the point of acceptance, the lies start to peel away. Reality is no longer denied and the truth comes out: Our bad circumstance (such as being overweight) is not about the past or about the temporary relief and comfort found in a bad habit (such as overeating). *It is about right now and what we choose to do with it.* A problem either continues to get worse or it becomes better with the next choice made. Take note—no matter what path was chosen before, choosing differently *now* is the key to losing our burdens for life.

This is your problem, and no one else is going to fix it for you. When you decide to change, it is going to be painful. No one can walk through that pain but you, and you must walk through it.

*Call to Me, and I will answer you, and show you great
and mighty things, which you do not know.*

Jeremiah 33:3

ACCEPTANCE

25

LOSE THE FEAR OF PAIN . . . GAIN THE FREEDOM OF FACING IT

I am suffering and in pain.
Rescue me, O God, by your saving power.
Psalm 69:29 NLT

Physical pain is necessary to our functioning. It is part of God's design for our bodies because it signals there is a problem to which we should attend. Emotional pain is similar. It signals there is a problem God wants to heal. When we see emotional pain as the symptom that leads us to depend on God and turn to Him for healing, we begin to understand its purpose.

Granted, you may be thinking, *If emotional pain is a gift, please don't give it to me!* But think about the times in your life when you have grown the most. Were they during the mountaintop experiences or in the lows of the valleys? Most of us grow during valley experiences, those difficult times in our lives when we can turn one of two ways—toward a more intimate relationship with God or away from Him. And when we choose to go to God, we grow and mature.

God is faithful and can be trusted. He may not always remove you from difficulty, but He promises His comfort, peace, and presence no matter what. No lifestyle, no matter how healthy, will free you from negative emotions or horrible pain, but you can find a way to face those moments, resolve them, and grow from the experience if you allow God to help you.

You might need to break a family pattern of avoidance by teaching your children to feel emotional pain and deal with it. What a gift to give the next generation! As your family learns to feel both the good and the bad, you will realize you can tolerate much more then you ever thought possible. No longer will your family have to hide from emotional feelings because you will have found freedom!

You can rely on God. He won't always protect you from horrible situations or difficult emotions, but He will always sustain and protect His children from hopelessness. God knows what you need every day in every circumstance. And through the pain and struggle of this journey, He will deliver you if you are willing.

One of the biggest barriers to moving forward in the things God has for us is getting stuck in our emotional pain and allowing it to move us away from God. When we experience trials or suffering, we might not loudly reject God, but we may very well begin to doubt who He is and whether He truly loves and cares for us. We all have experienced hurts and disappointments in our lives. For some of us, we've had deep traumas or abuse. For others, we've experienced lost dreams, disappointments, heartaches, and relationship problems. Certainly, there is no shortage of emotional pain. And unfortunately, all that suffering can lead us down the road to anxiety, depression, and other problems.

The reality is that putting our trust in anything or anyone but God will block our intimacy with Him. Our earthly supports, whether people or merchandise, gradually disappoint or fade away. We live in uncertain times. God wants us to look to Him first for security. He came to bring peace and comfort to those who mourn.

He has the power to heal the brokenhearted,
to proclaim liberty to the captive,
to open the prison doors to those who
are bound, to give beauty to ashes,
and the garment of praise
for the spirit of heaviness,
that we might be called trees of righteousness,
the planting of the Lord, *that He might be glorified.*
(adapted from Isaiah 61:1–3, emphasis added)

Let your emotional pain lead you to Him. Become His tree planted with deep roots, trusting Him, knowing Him, so that He can transform your pain for His glory. God wants you to come to Him no matter what—so don't allow your losses and pain to turn you away from Him. The answers are found in Him. "For in Him we live and move and have our being" (Acts 17:28).

Your loss might be the work of the enemy and something God allowed to happen. But just look at the story of Job. Job was righteous in God's eyes. He was faithful and yet lost everything because God allowed it. Job's story illustrates how we can obey God and be right in the center of His will and yet still experience great loss. And when this happens, it is very hard to understand, and harder still to accept.

Pour out your heart to the Lord as Hannah did in 1 Samuel 1. Remember that Christ has taken your grief and carried your sorrow (Isaiah 53). He identifies with what you are going through. He intimately knows every tear you cry, and He can handle your intense feelings.

In addition to pouring out your heart to God, find someone who will listen and who can be trusted with your pain. This might be a good friend, a counselor, a family member, or your spouse. The Bible instructs believers to "bear one another's burdens" (Galatians 6:2) and to intercede in prayer on behalf of others (James 5:16). Allow trusted people in your life to be a part of your healing journey. Often they have words of encouragement or scriptures that will uplift you and offer hope when you are feeling down.

Identify the feelings you have and then start to deal with them openly and honestly so the pain will no longer control any part of your life.

Those who sow in tears shall reap in joy.

Psalm 126:5

ACCEPTANCE

LOSE THE SICKNESS OF SECRECY . . . GAIN THE CLEANSING OF CONFESSION

[God] knows the secrets of the heart.

Psalm 44:21

Once you become more comfortable identifying feelings and allowing yourself to feel them, you need to be honest about what is going on inside you. There is sickness in secrecy. The sinning psalmist said, "When I kept things to myself, I felt weak deep inside me" (32:3 NCV). When we are willing to be open, healing becomes possible. By breaking our silence and speaking the truth about ourselves to another person, we move out of the darkness and bring secrets into the light. Confessing our sins and talking about the wrongs done to us is another key to spiritual healing and health.

CONFESSION

It is clearly important to God that men and women verbally express the struggles hidden in our hearts. Verbalization gives substance to inarticulate thoughts, and words affirm the realities of which we have become aware. Even on the key issue of Christian salvation, belief is to be affirmed with spoken words. Paul wrote, "If you confess with your mouth that Jesus is Lord and believe in your heart that God raised him from the dead, you will be saved. For it is by believing in your heart that you are made right with God, and it is by confessing with your mouth that you are saved" (Romans 10:9–10 NLT).

Unexpressed thoughts do not allow others to give input or challenge us to see the truth. When we confess our thoughts, we put others in the position of advising us, praying for us, and sharing our struggles. We must be careful, however: confession requires confidentiality. It is an invitation to intimacy and involves trust in both God and another person—a trust that is absolutely necessary for us to be able to truly reveal our secrets.

Openness is an outward act of trust that enables us to cleanse our souls from the inside out. If you want to be free from emotion–fueled burdens, such as overeating or overspending, you must confess the needs that are not being met and be honest about what you truly feel. Pretending not to have anger or not to be jealous will not help you heal, but honesty brings about authentic change. Confession means we:

* submit ourselves to God's ways of handling secrets.

* are willing to overcome our fear of rejection by revealing our failures to another person and admitting we need help from fellow believers.

* reject our habit of self–protective secretiveness.

* admit to at least one other person that we have fallen short of God's best, be it through character defects or judgment errors.

* stop trying to mask our true feelings and put our vague sense of guilt into written or spoken words, without making excuses.

By openly confessing our flaws and struggles, there is hope for healing. Admit what you really feel and where you struggle emotionally. Identify your hurts and losses. Do what James 5:16 commands: "Confess your sins to each other and pray for each other so that you can live together whole and healed" (MSG).

CONFESSION

Have more than one person to talk to about your struggles so you don't overburden anyone. Also, you won't feel guilty asking for help multiple times if you can spread around the need. Find someone who is a good listener, humble, trustworthy, evidences a quiet godliness, and is stable and positive. You want to avoid people with personal agendas or controlling personalities, as well as those who are needy, unstable, or sexually attractive to you. If you are married, it's better to find a same–sex confidante so that sexual tension will not be an issue. Lastly, remember to treat this person as a friend, not a therapist.

KEEP A PRAYER JOURNAL

You might want to keep a prayer journal, a tool to help document prayer requests and answers to prayer. This is also an excellent way to track your emotional swings. Whatever you feel, take it to God in prayer. Don't edit your feelings; just record them honestly. If you aren't sure how to begin, use this format and try this meaningful exercise:

1. Spend time in the Word or a devotional reading.
2. Write down a key verse or main idea from the reading.
3. Write out your prayer requests in response to what you have read.

CONFESSION

4. Spend time in prayer.

5. Wait for a personal word from the Lord. (This step takes time to develop.) Wait before the Lord in silence and allow Him to speak to you. Then write down what you believe you hear in your spirit. Don't be surprised if you think you don't hear anything at first. Most people report that it takes time to learn how to be quiet before the Lord and listen for His voice. With time, you will develop your spiritual hearing.

REPLACE YOUR BAD HABITS
WITH NEW BEHAVIORS

Pain is not optional, but misery is. You can't always control pain, but you can do something about misery. If you are looking for a quick fix to emotional pain, you're reading the wrong book! Healing is often progressive because it requires changes in your character and actions. The way you cope with emotional pain must change if you are going to make any positive change in your life.

Keeping a record of what you do when you become emotionally upset is a good way to watch your progress—perhaps in a journal. The journey to finding new alternatives to coping with pain might look like this:

CONFESSION

Event: Received an upsetting phone call

Emotion: Very hurt

Reaction: Gobbled some comfort food

Now, think of a new way to cope with that feeling. Here's another example:

Event: Heard someone gossip about me

Emotion: Anger

New Reaction: Gently confront the person who did the gossiping

To help yourself choose alternatives to an unhealthy response to pain, make a list of twenty behaviors you can use instead the next time you're hurt. Your list should include things you can do while driving, being at home, at work, or on the go. Post the list on your refrigerator and make a copy to take with you. Every time you're tempted to react negatively because you feel an unpleasant emotion, pull out your list and choose a new thing to do. Feel free to borrow ideas from this list:

1. Take a short walk and cool down.
2. Listen to calming music.
3. Take three deep breaths.
4. Distract yourself with something in the room or car.
5. Take a bubble bath.

6. Call a friend.
7. Count to 20.
8. Take a short nap.
9. Pray and ask God to help you.
10. Turn up the radio and get lost in the music.
11. Stand up and do some stretches.
12. Go to the bathroom, even if it's only to splash water on your face.
13. Play with your dog.
14. Play with your child.
15. Watch a funny movie.
16. Go somewhere quiet and practice deep muscle relaxation.
17. Clean something.
18. Run up and down the stairs to release tension.
19. Work on a crossword or sudoku puzzle.
20. Play a video game.

Maybe you've been hurt by a divorce, an abusive parent, a betraying friend, or an insulting boss. Whatever the cause of your hurt, it's time to throw away your emotional crutches and let the pain surface. When you do, you might experience intense feelings of anger or fear, but there will not be healing until you face those feelings.

CONFESSION

Just let the feelings come, and ask God to help you understand exactly why you feel as you do. Don't try to edit your thoughts. Whatever comes into your mind, grab that thought. Most likely you've accepted some lies that were implanted at the time of the emotional pain when you first experienced those feelings. Try to identify the lies, and once you find them, ask Jesus to speak His truth to you. Wait and listen for His voice, whether it comes in the form of a whisper of His Spirit or a visual picture He may give you. Wait on Him and expect Him to bring truth. His truth brings release from the lies.

For you were once darkness, but now you are light in the Lord.
Walk as children of light (for the fruit of the Spirit is in all goodness, righteousness,
and truth), finding out what is acceptable to the Lord.
And have no fellowship with the unfruitful works of darkness,
but rather expose them. For it is shameful even to speak of those things
which are done by them in secret. But all things that are exposed
are made manifest by the light, for whatever makes manifest is light.
Therefore He says: "Awake, you who sleep,
arise from the dead, and Christ will give you light."

Ephesians 5:8–14

CONFESSION

LOSE THE EMPTINESS OF SELF ... GAIN THE FULLNESS OF GOD

I hated life. It made me sad to think that everything here on earth is useless, like chasing the wind. . . . What do people get for all their work and struggling here on earth? All of their lives their work is full of pain and sorrow, and even at night their minds don't rest. This is also useless.

Ecclesiastes 2:17, 22—23 NCV

I always had difficulty keeping off weight because of two disconnection factors: disconnection from God and disconnection from others. I was an independent loner and rather than work through this chronic problem, I prided myself on my identity. The emptiness of my life drove me back to food over and over again. Although a diet worked to take my weight off, it didn't keep it off. That state of being only came when I

CONFESSION

put into place the other factors that would fill my emptiness and heal the emotional conflicts I was experiencing. To keep the weight off—or to make any other positive life change—eventually you have to fill your emptiness with something other than self-indulgence and start to resolve the emotions.

We can feel empty because of unmet emotional needs. Another reason is because we have no active, living relationship with God. We don't go to God with our hurts as He instructs us to do. We don't call on Him for help when we feel helpless. Or we don't trust Him to help us handle our difficult feelings, and so we indulge in activities that cover the pain.

Our culture rarely suggests God as an answer to combating feelings of emptiness. Instead, it promotes materialism and false solutions. It tells us we need more—more food, more sex, more cars, bigger homes—more and more, bigger and bigger! The message is shouted, advertised, sold, and publicized again and again: *More stuff is the answer to your longings.* Empty? Get more!

The truth is that only a personal, intimate relationship with God can satisfy the emptiness we feel. We were created to want more of God. Apart from God, we won't find satisfaction. And He doesn't leave us without a way to satisfy that longing

(Matthew 7:7–8). In addition, the emptiness must be filled with caring people who can love and support us through difficulty. Filling up with things is a poor substitute for relationships and intimacy. Through community and relationships we meet our needs for love and intimacy. We cannot do it alone.

You have not seen Christ, but still you love him.
You cannot see him now, but you believe in him.
So you are filled with a joy that cannot be explained, a joy full of glory.

1 Peter 1:8 NCV

CONFESSION

LOSE THE EXCUSES . . . GAIN ACCEPTANCE OF RESPONSIBLITY

❧

Each person must be responsible for himself.
Galatians 6:5 NCV

❧

All of us struggle with blind spots in our lives, and to some degree we all live in the company of denial and self–deception. But rather than confront our area(s) of struggle and pain, we often point to others and focus on them or find alternatives to distract and anesthetize ourselves from what really needs to be faced.

Making excuses is perhaps the most common way to justify a bad habit and deal with failure. With a good excuse, guilt and anxiety about a problem dissipate. But the sad reality is that your excuses are a big part of your problem. Happily, there is an alternative, but first you must see excuses for what they really are.

Acceptance is being willing to lift the curtain of denial and look at the big lie of your life. Breaking through denial means being aware of your struggle and pain and consciously confronting the behaviors and patterns that have deterred you from God's best. Only with God's help and a supportive, healing community can the blinders be removed.

Deception and denial give way to seeing yourself as you really are—trapped in your patterns, paralyzed by fear, and making choices that produce short–term results rather than long–term change. God is patient, loving, and "able to do far more than we would ever dare to ask or even dream of—infinitely beyond our highest prayers, desires, thoughts, or hopes" (Ephesians 3:20 TLB). Take a moment and examine your heart. How have you avoided reality? See if any of these actions play a role in how you avoid the truth:

* You avoid prayer, times of silence, and looking at your situation, honest conversations that touch a sensitive area of your life, or people who can speak into your life and encourage you on your journey.

❋ You minimize or rationalize your behavior.

❋ You constantly criticize others.

❋ You are confused as to why others react to you and what you say or do.

❋ You find yourself lying repeatedly.

If you are willing to confront the realities of your life, these positive signs will be evident:

❋ You focus on what you can do to change rather than on what you want others to do to make you feel better.

❋ You humble yourself in order to confront who you really are.

❋ You look for what really causes the conflicts you experience.

❋ You honestly face your past pain and failures head on.

❋ You stop blaming others for your difficulties.

❋ You see, receive, and apply God's wisdom to your situation.

* You look at what you've done in the light of God's mercy and grace—not judgment or condemnation.

* You accept that you are unable to help yourself without God's help.

* You can name your character defects and mistakes rather than deny them.

By being honest you can move out of the past and into the reality of the present. Only when you face the truth can God teach you to resolve your problems rather than reproduce them within relationships with family and close friends.

Blessed is the man who endures temptation; for when he has been approved, he will receive the crown of life which the Lord has promised to those who love Him. Let no one say when he is tempted, "I am tempted by God"; for God cannot be tempted by evil, nor does He Himself tempt anyone. But each one is tempted when he is drawn away by his own desires and enticed. Then, when desire has conceived, it gives birth to sin; and sin, when it is full-grown, brings forth death.

James 1:12—15

RESPONSIBILITY

LOSE THE URGE TO INDULGE...
GAIN SELF-CONTROL

Moderation is better than muscle, self–control better than political power.

Proverbs 16:32 MSG

A dvertisers sell immediate gratification. Their job is to persuade you to be impulsive, to give in to temptation.

To make any positive change in your life requires you to delay momentary gratification and think with a long–term perspective—to engage in the reality of your decisions. When you are tempted to succumb to an immediate pleasure, think about the impact of this one choice on your life. Ask yourself questions like these:

❋ How will I feel immediately after I do this?

❋ How will I feel in thirty minutes?

✷   How will I feel about this tomorrow morning?

✷   Will I beat myself up over this choice?

You get the idea. To beat the habit, don't rationalize what you are doing. Think about the long-term consequences, and learn to tolerate your anxious feelings, which generally will pass after only a short time. Take a few deep breaths and relax your body; the urge to indulge will likely subside within twenty minutes or so. Or you can distract yourself by listening to music, reading a book, calling a friend, taking a walk, going for a drive, attending a meeting, or just going to bed. Whatever you do, don't just stare at temptation and try to exercise willpower. These strategies work for any impulsive behavior, including overeating and overspending.

Delaying gratification is a process that involves self-control, one of the fruits of the Spirit (Galatians 5:22–23). Just as fruit begins with a seed, so too does a fruitful spiritual life. Both need nourishment to thrive. We need to read the Word of God and let it soak very deep into our hearts. The more we desire to please God in all we do, the more obedient we become. Obedience produces self-discipline, which gives way to self-control. We are not talking about control born of self-effort, but self-control born of the Spirit working in us.

The enemy of our souls wants to discourage us from ever thinking we could have a supernatural self–control. Satan even tested Jesus in the wilderness. This fallen angel came to Jesus when He was physically weak, hungry, and tired from fasting. Satan, knowing the toll of hunger on Jesus' earthly body, suggested a shortcut—an immediate gratification. However, the biblical account begins with an important fact: *the Spirit* led Jesus into the wilderness (Matthew 4:1; Luke 4:1). Don't miss the importance of this—being led by the Spirit is what we all need in order to overcome our weaknesses.

And Jesus' defense against succumbing to immediate gratification was to quote Scripture to His enemy. The Living Word quoted the Word. This is your model for overcoming. As you soak yourself in the Word, you nourish your spiritual life. The seed bears fruit—in this case, self–control. Be ready for times of testing. Nourish yourself with plenty of time in the Word and allow your life to bear the fruit of the Spirit.

Let your moderation be known unto all men. The Lord is at hand.

Philippians 4:5 KJV

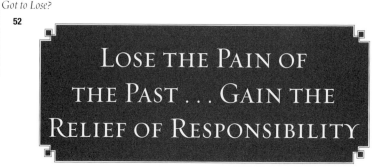

LOSE THE PAIN OF THE PAST … GAIN THE RELIEF OF RESPONSIBILITY

Take heed to yourself, and diligently keep yourself, lest you forget the things your eyes have seen, and lest they depart from your heart all the days of your life.

Deuteronomy 4:9

Another key element of a life no longer controlled by bad habits or extra baggage is a newfound sense of responsibility. We must refuse to blame anyone else for our problems and acknowledge that we are responsible, yet we can't fix this on our own power. This is the balance of surrendering to God: we allow God to do what we cannot do, but we do what we can.

Responsibility involves the treatment of old wounds that may be triggering your negative behaviors. It also requires making strong decisions and changes in your life. Hurts that drive you to inappropriate behaviors and destructive habits are hurts that you may never have worked through. Diverting yourself from problems or anesthetizing your emotions with overeating, being around hurtful people, or burying yourself in activities may be a common pattern in your life.

In this world, it's easy to take on the role of victim and live a life of victimization. Yet as horrendous as your past problems and abuse may have been, when you own them as part of yourself, you learn to see them as purposeful, deepening, and integral to your development of godly character. It takes courage to walk through this pain, but God can provide the strength and support to truly overcome past hurts and, ultimately, to use them for His glory. As the psalmist David wrote, "It was good for me to suffer so I would learn your demands" (Psalm 119:71 NCV).

Avoiding pain and problems is a natural human response. Most people feel they have "suffered enough" and have no desire to feel overwhelmed by sorrowful emotions. But grief is a necessary process of this earthly life, because we all fail, suffer, and deal with loss. It is important to note that experiencing grief over our failures and losses connects us to God's grace. Saint Augustine affirmed this when he said, "In my deepest wound I saw your glory and it dazzled me." It is not pleasant, but it is necessary. We must experience (or grieve) the pain we feel today so we will not be driven by it in the future. Too often we point to our past pain as an excuse and miss the fact that it very definitely is part of God's plan for us. It is so easy to blame others for everything that has gone wrong. When we don't accept responsibility, we live in a victimized state and blame others for our problems.

Inevitably, people who try to change their lives come to a crossroads where they must decide whether to face the emotional pain fueling their behaviors or ignore the underlying issues and revert to old habits. The amazing thing is that people who face their wounds can be healed. The men and women they were created to be can and will surface. They will be living proof of the grace of God.

GOD sent me to announce the year of his grace—

a celebration of God's destruction of our enemies—

and to comfort all who mourn,

To care for the needs of all who mourn in Zion,

give them bouquets of roses instead of ashes,

Messages of joy instead of news of doom,

a praising heart instead of a languid spirit.

Rename them "Oaks of Righteousness"

planted by GOD to display his glory.

Isaiah 61:2–3 MSG

LOSE THE GOOD INTENTIONS . . . GAIN THE TOOLS FOR GODLY ACTIONS

*Seek first the kingdom of God and His righteousness,
and all these things shall be added to you.*

Matthew 6:33

E ver notice how good intentions don't always bring success?
The reality is that action is required to achieve goals.

Faith is the belief or confidence that God will do all He says
He will do. As we read God's Word and implant it deep in our
hearts, action must follow what we read and hear. James confirms
this in his epistle (1:22–25):

Do what God's teaching says; when you only listen and
do nothing, you are fooling yourselves. Those who hear God's

teaching and do nothing are like people who look at themselves in a mirror. They see their faces and then go away and quickly forget what they looked like. But the truly happy people are those who carefully study God's perfect law that makes people free, and they continue to study it. They do not forget what they heard, but they obey what God's teaching says. Those who do this will be made happy (NCV).

Don't you want to be that person who finds delight and affirmation in action? With the Holy Spirit operating in your life, you are empowered to do those things you know to be true. God has already given you what you need to overcome. When you confess Christ as your Savior, the Holy Spirit takes up residence in you. It is His presence that empowers each of us to overcome.

TOOLS FOR CHANGE

Change is a process that involves multiple steps. Below is an outline of six steps necessary to bring change to your life.

1. Illumination. When you see the need for change, you have reached illumination. As Paul wrote, "You groped your way through that murk once, but no longer. You're out in the open now. The bright light of Christ makes your way plain. So no more stumbling around. Get on with it!" (Ephesians 5:8 MSG).

2. Inspiration. Once you see the need for change, you must be inspired to make necessary changes. Ask God for His help and guidance. Change may be needed in several areas of your life—eating healthier, exercising more, dealing better with your emotions, or thinking and acting in more positive ways. Ask God for the courage to change and be transformed into what is God's best for you. See what you can become and become motivated by the vision.

3. Examination. As we are inspired to make changes, we must take a good hard look at how we measure up to God's standards. Do you imitate Christ in all you do? Are you living a holy life? Are you obedient to the Word? Whatever your answers are to these questions, you can begin today to evaluate your life according to God's Word. No one is perfect, but after examining your life closely, you should be more inclined to want to live in obedience to God's Word.

4. Motivation. When you understand that the life God has for you is beyond what you could even imagine, you have reached the step of motivation. Walking in His truth and staying obedient to His Word are your secret weapons to developing a purposeful life. Ask the Holy Spirit to fill you so full of Him that something beyond yourself will happen. The more we seek the kingdom of God and all His righteousness, the more used of God we will be. If you have struggled with motivation for years, perhaps it is time to realize that you just don't have the ability to motivate yourself. But you can reach out to someone else; you can bring people around you to help coach you and provide you with the motivation you do not possess on your own. That is what God has in mind when we surround ourselves with a body of believers.

5. Determination. No matter what you've been through already, don't give up. If you fall down and blow it, get up and try again. God gives us second chances. He wants us to succeed. With Christ, all things are possible (Philippians 4:13). Stay in the fight and keep reaching for the prize.

6. Realization. Supernatural things can happen. Persevere until change comes, and be of good courage. You are a champion because of God's ability to change people. Your life matters and God has plans for you. James 1:12 says, "Blessed is the man who perseveres under trial, because when he has stood the test, he will receive the crown of life that God has promised to those who love him" (NIV).

> Let your eyes look straight ahead,
> And your eyelids look right before you.
> Ponder the path of your feet,
> And let all your ways be established.
> Do not turn to the right or the left;
> Remove your foot from evil.
>
> Proverbs 4:25—27

RESPONSIBILITY

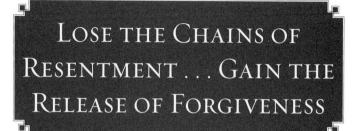

LOSE THE CHAINS OF RESENTMENT ... GAIN THE RELEASE OF FORGIVENESS

Love your enemies, . . .
be merciful, just as your Father also is merciful.
Judge not, and you shall not be judged.
Condemn not, and you shall not be condemned.
Forgive, and you will be forgiven.

Luke 6:35–37

A s we surrender our lives to God, another action becomes
necessary: forgiveness. Throughout the Word, Jesus is very
specific about our need to forgive. "If you forgive men when
they sin against you, your heavenly Father will also forgive you"
(Matthew 6:14 NIV). This is stated as a contingency, meaning
we have an active part to accomplish as well as the action of our
heavenly Father forgiving us.

Forgiveness, when empowered by God's Spirit, is a process of detaching painful events from our emotional responses to them, thus facilitating the process of healing. When we forgive, we recognize our own failures and are humbled. To forgive and receive forgiveness are gracious acts of love. These acts have supernatural power to change both the life of the forgiven and the one who forgives. When we look at how God has forgiven us, it moves us to find a way to forgive others even if they have deeply hurt us. Only the cross of Christ makes forgiveness possible.

Forgiveness is inextricably interwoven into Christian salvation. Jesus clearly taught that unless we forgive others, our heavenly Father cannot forgive us. At first glance, this may appear to be a rigid and rigorous principle, but it is God's means of extending His grace to everyone. When we refuse to forgive, we play "god" in the lives of others and pass our judgment on to them. This interferes with the process of grace Jesus Christ initiated at the cross. Forgiveness means:

* we return our rights to God (the rights we usurped from Him when we became disobedient) and invite Him to be in charge.

* we obey Jesus' instructions to forgive, and in turn we can be forgiven.

FORGIVENESS

✳ we no longer energize ourselves with rage or hatred over events or feelings from the past.

✳ we stop trying to change other people and ask God to do it.

✳ we begin a process of restitution to right whatever wrongs we may have caused.

Forgiveness can be difficult—almost impossible—for those who have been abused physically, sexually, or even spiritually. It is never easy or instant; it may, in fact, take years to complete. However, if forgiveness isn't rendered, injured people remain trapped in the abuse of the past where they endlessly relive the offenses done against them. Our yesterdays must be put in the past so we can fully enjoy today.

The forgiveness process also involves making things right with those we have wounded. This may require us to write letters or make phone calls, to repay debts, or to make amends or otherwise do our part in making wrongs as right as possible. This, of course, can result in enormous spiritual blessings, both for others and for ourselves.

Don't underestimate the fact that forgiveness is difficult. To succeed, we all need the help of family or friends as well as God. Don't be an island determined to do this all alone. Let others come alongside and encourage you. Humble yourself before the Lord and acknowledge your need of Him, and He will lift you up (James 4:10).

Often it is painful to change our hearts and our behaviors. When we have been wronged, it is so much easier to break off all contact and not have a relationship with the person who hurt us. Yet this isn't what God asks us to do. We must move beyond our pain and take the path of forgiveness, as Christ forgave us.

God sees your heart and knows if you are sincere. He will help you move through the process of forgiveness if you desire to do so. It may help to make a list of those grudges and offenses you have held onto and would like to release. Then, take each item and pray, asking the Lord to forgive you or the person who hurt you. Releasing these burdens is powerful in the battle to change yourself. You cannot skip this step and still succeed. Take the time, examine your heart, and ask God to show you if there is hidden resentment or judgment. Seek release today.

For You, Lord, are good, and ready to forgive,
And abundant in mercy to all those who call upon You.

Psalm 86:5

LOSE THE IDOLATRY OF THE BODY ... GAIN A WORSHIPFUL BEING

Thus says the LORD:
"Let not the wise man glory in his wisdom,
Let not the mighty man glory in his might,
Nor let the rich man glory in his riches;
But let him who glories glory in this,
That he understands and knows Me,
That I am the LORD, exercising lovingkindness,
judgment, and righteousness in the earth.
For in these I delight," says the LORD.

Jeremiah 9:23–24

Your body is valuable. After all, God created it. He chose you as His, and you are a vessel for His Spirit. Read 1 Corinthians 6:19: "Or didn't you realize that your body is a sacred

place, the place of the Holy Spirit? Don't you see that you can't
live however you please, squandering what God paid such a high
price for? The physical part of you is not some piece of property
belonging to the spiritual part of you" (MSG).

Our bodies are sacred and what we do with them affects all
parts of us. Our bodies are the dwelling places of the Most High
God. We need to take care of them and allow them to be used
for God's glory. If gluttony or sex or violence or other physical
manifestation of sin is what prevents us from being used for
God's glory, we need to admit it and repent from it, however
painful that act may be. Transformation will only occur when we
face the reality of what we are involved in.

However, our interest in our bodies can take on an idol-
worshiplike proportion. When we worry, think, and obsess about
what we will eat, or look forward to meals more than our time
with God, we are out of balance. Worry is a distracting trait.

A life decided for God has the promise that God will meet
your physical needs as well as your emotional and spiritual ones.
Accept the promises. God wants you to enjoy eating yet not
become a glutton. He wants you to enjoy sex yet not outside the
sanctity of marriage. He wants you to enjoy physical strength yet

not for the purpose of intimidating or harming others. Anything taken to excess—even the striving for a healthy lifestyle—can block a vibrant relationship with God. Moderation is key.

The Bible tells us to get out of spiritual poverty by developing self-control, a fruit of the Spirit (Galatians 5:23), and to submit our entire lives to God "as living sacrifices" (Romans 12:1). Allow Him to use you for His glory—it is a primary reason for why you were created!

We have other needs apart from our physical bodies. We need to be safe, to belong, to be loved, to be esteemed, and to grow. When something stirs our emotions—and we feel happy, sad, depressed, angry, and the like—we may be triggered to use our bodies to respond in physical ways. We must be aware of our emotional connection to our bodies and discipline ourselves to keep our actions in line with God's will. Our emotions may tell us that our bodies need comfort— through food, sex, entertainment, whatever—but our obedient spirits must be in charge of dealing with our needs.

Beth Moore says, "Victory is not determined as much by what we've been delivered from as by what we've been delivered to." She is so right. God wants to deliver you. He wants you to find your purpose, move in His power, and live a life of overcoming.

He offers Himself to you. He is your deliverer. With God there is relationship, intimacy, abundant life, peace, joy, and so much more! He offers that which will satisfy. Heed His promise! He wants you, chose you, and is waiting to fill your life with good things (Psalm 84:11).

When you feel depressed by a gnawing emptiness in your soul, focus on your hope in Christ. God's promises are many, and they are meant to be read and treasured and cried over and praised over. Let these scriptures encourage you and fill that empty space within you.

For whatever things were written before were written for our learning, that we through the patience and comfort of the Scriptures might have hope.
Romans 15:4

Now may the God of hope fill you with all joy and peace in believing, that you may abound in hope by the power of the Holy Spirit.
Romans 15:13

The eyes of your understanding being enlightened; that you may know what is the hope of His calling, what are the riches of the glory of His inheritance in the saints.
Ephesians 1:18

TRANSFORMATION

God has so much more for you. He doesn't want you dragging through life being defeated. He wants to give you good things—more of His power, more of His Spirit, more of His love and compassion. Are you afraid you won't get what you need? Not to worry. God has enough to go around for all of us. His resources are limitless. He is the Living Water that never runs dry. He is the Bread of Life who promises eternal life. The fullness He has for you cannot be found in the temporal things of this world. And once you experience His fullness, you'll never hunger in the same way again!

So why don't we hunger and thirst after righteousness? Too often it is because we listen to the voice of the accuser. The Bible tells us the accuser is the devil and that he accuses us day and night (Revelation 12:10). Think about it. Satan can't undo our salvation, so he has to have other tricks to trip us up. One of his best schemes is to accuse us with claims that we aren't worthy, we can't lose weight, or that we are all losers. His accusations are constantly ringing in our ears. But we cannot listen to him or believe his lies because we have been cleared of all accusations, as Hebrews 10:19–23 tells us:

So, brothers and sisters, we are completely free to enter the Most Holy Place without fear because of the blood of Jesus' death.

We can enter through a new and living way that Jesus opened for us. It leads through the curtain—Christ's body. And since we have a great priest over God's house, let us come near to God with a sincere heart and a sure faith, because we have been made free from a guilty conscience, and our bodies have been washed with pure water. Let us hold firmly to the hope that we have confessed, because we can trust God to do what he promised (NCV).

Did you grasp that truth? You are cleansed by the blood of Christ's sacrifice. Once you confess sin, there is nothing Satan can do about it because it's no longer there. So he can accuse all he wants. You just tell him to go take a hike because there is nothing left for Satan to accuse. You have to believe this truth and stop letting the devil take your past and hold it up like an autobiography. Yes, you have sinned, but once confessed, the book's pages are blank. There is no record of those wrongs anymore, because the sin has been cleared.

You've got to get this into your spirit and not allow the enemy to steal your joy. Hunger for more of God. God holds all satisfaction. Perhaps you've tried to find satisfaction in many other ways. Rest in the assurance that nothing completely satisfies except more of God. God wants to fill your hungry, empty life with the bread that truly satisfies, and He will—when you sit down for the meal and open your heart and life to His will and His voice.

Since you died with Christ and were made free from the ruling spirits of the world, why do you act as if you still belong to this world by following rules like these: "Don't eat this," "Don't taste that," "Don't even touch that thing"? These rules refer to earthly things that are gone as soon as they are used. They are only man—made commands and teachings. They seem to be wise, but they are only part of a man—made religion. They make people pretend not to be proud and make them punish their bodies, but they do not really control the evil desires of the sinful self. Since you were raised from the dead with Christ, aim at what is in heaven, where Christ is sitting at the right hand of God. Think only about the things in heaven, not the things on earth. Your old sinful self has died, and your new life is kept with Christ in God. Christ is our life, and when he comes again, you will share in his glory.

Colossians 2:20—3:4 NCV

TRANSFORMATION

LOSE THE UNHEALTHY SELF-IMAGE ... GAIN A MENTAL MAKEOVER

I will praise You, for I am fearfully and wonderfully made;
Marvelous are Your works, And that my soul knows very well.

Psalm 139:14

We all need a makeover—an internal one. If you struggle with negative self–image, the solution is surgery within the heart. The results last a lifetime, and the transformation that comes from being the bride of Christ is beyond any physical makeover one could ever experience. It is extreme, life changing, and affirming—"But we all, with unveiled face, beholding as in a mirror the glory of the Lord, are being transformed into the same image from glory to glory, just as by the Spirit of the Lord" (2 Corinthians 3:18).

TRANSFORMATION

How does such a makeover happen? One important step in the process is the renewing of your mind, or changing how you view yourself, God, and others. To start, let us address these three key areas.

BODY IMAGE

Whose image do we reflect? In Genesis 1:26–27, God explains that we are made in His image and reflect His likeness. He declared His created design "good," meaning that nothing about our bodies is a mistake. However, we do make mistakes when we don't take care of our bodies. Eating too much food and getting too little exercise are actually abuses against the human body that are a direct result of the human will. Our bodies are not our enemies; our wills are.

IDENTITY

Our acceptance, security, and significance are to be found in Christ. If we look to any other source for our true identity, we'll be disappointed by the result. The root of all image problems is related to identity. Our identities must be fully secure in Christ. We belong to Him, and we must not allow ourselves to be defined otherwise.

WORTH

God's love for us has nothing to do with appearance or weight. We are His beloved, and we are valued and esteemed because of Him, not because of the way we look. He looks at our hearts and wants to capture them. We were bought with a price: the precious blood of the Lamb. Value is determined by how much someone is willing to pay for it. Christ obviously values each of us a great deal in that He gave His life for us.

Your perspective regarding your body, identity, and worth may require new focus as you meditate on God's Word and learn more specifically how God thinks about you. If you doubt these truths, then your mind is in need of renewal.

Negative body image is like a modern plague that continues to torment us. But it doesn't have to be. We can resist cultural prescriptions and renew our minds with biblical thought. Our bodies are the dwelling place of the Holy Spirit (1 Corinthians 3:16), literally holy temples!

TRANSFORMATION

There is a healthy balance between body obsession and hating our bodies. Somewhere in the middle is acceptance and responsibility. The way you think about your body will be reflected externally. Proverbs 23:7 says, "For as he thinks in his heart, so is he." Hence, you are what you think. Yet to hate your body is to reject the beautiful creation God has made in His image. Instead, you must accept your body, flaws and all, and take care of that holy temple. Five key steps to accepting your body are:

1. Stop degrading your body. Negative statements about yourself lead to negative feelings. You would not say such things about a friend, and you shouldn't talk about yourself this way either. Become your best encourager rather than your worst critic. Instead of thinking, *I'm ugly and undesirable,* tell yourself *I'm overweight but I'm working on it.*

2. Stop putting life on hold because you don't like your body. Do what you love to do. Live in the present reality even as you implement changes for the future.

3. Think of good things to say about yourself. You are more than your weight or your hair or your wrinkles. Focus on the positive qualities you have that can be emphasized.

TRANSFORMATION

4. Develop your own style and personality. Not everyone judges you by your appearance. Take a chance and reach out to others rather than hiding behind your perceived flaws. Let your true personality shine.

5. Get your esteem from God. Self–esteem is a misleading term. None of us can truly have esteem by looking to the *self.* The *self* is sinful, self–centered, and easily deceived. God esteems you just because He chose you and loves you. You don't have to earn His esteem; you already have it. Remember, He values you so much that He gave His only Son to die for you.

Thoughts lead to feelings. Feelings lead to actions. Actions influence our perceptions, which then influence our thoughts. It's a vicious cycle. What we think affects how we feel, which affects how we respond. Thus, many negative feelings can be avoided by changing the thought that prompts the feeling. If, for example, I feel sad because I purposely think, *Nobody cares about me,* I can change my sad feelings by changing the thought to a more positive and realistic one—*God cares about me even when others don't.* Because this thought is reassuring and doesn't make me feel sad, I'm unlikely to respond in a negative way.

We must RISE to a new level of thinking.

Reduce negative thoughts and self–degrading statements.

Increase our awareness of God and our esteem and acceptance of the bodies we were given.

Substitute positive thoughts for negative ones.

Eliminate errors and lies from our thinking.

You were bought at a price; therefore glorify God in your body and in your spirit, which are God's.

1 Corinthians 6:20

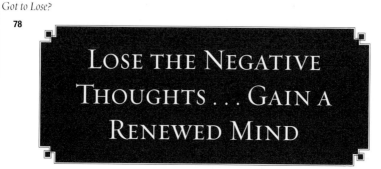

LOSE THE NEGATIVE THOUGHTS ... GAIN A RENEWED MIND

A merry heart does good, like medicine,
But a broken spirit dries the bones.

Proverbs 17:22

The word "renew" means a change of heart and life. It is work the Holy Spirit does in us. As we offer our bodies as a living sacrifice to God (Romans 12:1), we allow the Holy Spirit to radically work in our hearts and minds. Renewing the mind is different from positive thinking in that truth must be experienced from the One who is truth.

Whenever something negative or traumatic happens to us, the enemy uses those circumstances to implant a lie, because his plan is to deceive us about who God is. During times of emotional pain, he tries hard to seduce us away from God's truth and into a pit of darkness. If we don't know the truth, or we let down our spiritual guard, we can accept his lies in place of truth.

So much of the pain and turmoil we feel today has to do with lies implanted from times when we experienced hurt and were wounded. We believe we are hopeless, that God doesn't care, that people are always letting us down. And although none of these statements is true, we adjust our reality to make them come true.

Although we are saved and our spirits are made new in Christ (2 Corinthians 5:17), our minds are still in need of renewal. Yet we cannot be free of the lies and distorted thinking on our own power. A renewed mind comes as we receive truth from Christ and deeply plant His Word in our hearts.

How many times have you known something to be true, such as, "God loves me and would never leave me," yet you *feel* this isn't true? Your experience tells you that what you know to be true isn't true. And here is the great disconnect: You can know truth in your head but not have it connect to your heart. You need an experience of truth to make it real to you and connect your head and heart. That's where prayer comes in. When you know your heart says one thing and your head says another, ask Christ to speak His truth to you. Read His Word and ask Him to penetrate it deep into your mind and soul. Look at the Gospels. Do you notice that Jesus healed (an experience) and then spoke to the person (cognitive)? The Truth gave truth, both experientially and cognitively.

Identify the lies that create your emotional pain. Lies can come to us by the words of others, by our own perceptions, or during times of hurt and trauma. Once you identify a lie, ask Christ to speak His truth.

Perhaps the biggest lie we tell ourselves is that all we can do about our problem is pray to God to get rid of it. And although this might be true, and we can pray that prayer, the answer is often going to require more than waiting for God. Or God may choose not to take away this burden, which is often the case.

Whether or not you have a life of meaning and purpose or stagnation and death is quite often dependent on what you are willing to change. You wait for God to do what God is waiting for you to do. Why? Because God wants to build your character, and the way He does that is by sticking with you through a struggle, gently supporting your efforts if they are honorable and glorify Him.

TRANSFORMATION

TAKE THE NEGATIVE THOUGHTS CAPTIVE

In 2 Corinthians 10:5 we are told to take our thoughts captive: "We use our powerful God–tools for smashing warped philosophies, tearing down barriers erected against the truth of God, fitting every loose thought and emotion and impulse into the structure of life shaped by Christ" (MSG).

If you grew up in a home in which you were constantly criticized, negative thoughts have been deeply ingrained. Don't worry. You can renew your mind with the help of God and others.

To apply this scripture, you must be aware of what you are thinking. Once you realize the thought is negative, self– degrading, or untrue, you should stop the thought. To stop a thought, pretend you are grabbing it out of the air. You have now taken it captive. Now you need to smash it or replace it with a thought that is true, one that fits a life shaped by Christ.

You have to gain control of your thoughts. And with practice you can do this. Sometimes it helps to put a rubber band on your wrist and snap it every time you tell yourself a negative thought or lie. The mild pain is a simple reminder to grab the negative thought. Until you do something like this, you may not realize how many times a day negative thoughts race through your mind. Like spam mail on a computer, the thoughts just show up and keep on coming. As with email, the trick is not to click on the thoughts to open them. Instead, delete them instantly and avoid giving negative thoughts a foothold in your mind, because they are messages of Satan, not God.

THE ANSWER FOR NEGATIVE THOUGHTS

"I'm just anxious; I'm not thinking anything." Wrong! You have thoughts behind those anxious feelings. The feelings may be so intense that you aren't aware of the self–talk that preceded your anxiety, but such talk is behind most anxious feelings. Remember, your thoughts impact your feelings.

Anxious thoughts are automatic for people with anxiety problems. A person may feel anxious and yet be unaware of preceding thoughts. The first step is to identify your thought before the anxious feeling occurs, although the thought won't always be obvious. Self–talk can spawn and reinforce anxious feelings or it can dismiss anxiety and build confidence. Self–talk is that powerful. When lies and negative thoughts become frequent, they create and sustain anxiety. Anxious people think in ways that perpetuate anxiety. Review this checklist and find out if you think like an anxious person.

AM I ANXIOUS?

1.   *It's going to be a catastrophe!* You think of extremely negative consequences and assume it's going to happen.

2.   *It's personal!* Whatever happens around you is somehow personally relevant and will most likely happen to you next. For example, if there's a fire in the city, your house is next.

3.   *It could happen!* You magnify the one part of the issue that could create a problem and ignore the nonthreatening parts.

4.   *It doesn't matter what else is going on. I see danger.* You ignore the context of a problem and choose to focus on the one thing that could be dangerous or problematic, no matter how unlikely it is.

5.   *I can tell this is trouble!* At any sign of trouble, you immediately jump to conclusions. For example, air turbulence means the plane is crashing.

6.   *I can't. I don't have what it takes. I won't be able to do it.* You believe nothing will change and you can't meet the challenge. You have given up before starting and aren't asking God to help you overcome your weakness.

7.   *It will happen again.* You overgeneralize to the next situation and assume something bad will happen next time just because it happened before.

8.   *It's all or nothing.* You believe things happen all the time or not at all. You see only black and white, not gray. All–or–nothing thinkers are often disappointed and need to build tolerance for failure and imperfection.

9.   *Perfection is required.* You keep thinking *I should have . . .* or *I have to . . .* You always worry about your failures, and you don't allow for mistakes or human fallibility.

10.   *It's going to be bad.* You are far too critical and need to give yourself a break. You need a shot of God–esteem. Your classic thoughts are: *I can't believe I did that. How stupid. What an idiot I am.*

11.   *What about . . . ?* You are the classic worrier. Nothing can happen without you fearing all the possibilities for disaster or problems. You fail to realize that you really don't have control.

Worrying about everything that can go wrong is sin. God tells us to be anxious about nothing. He wants us to hand over the worry to Him. He will take care of us no matter what.

If you related to these statements, you need to change your thoughts. Write down positive statements that will counter the negative ones, and use scriptures to back up your new positions.

Here's a powerful scripture you can always use: "I can do all things through Christ who strengthens me" (Philippians 4:13). The next time you feel anxious, stop and ask yourself what thought is making you feel that way. Chances are it's a negative thought that needs changing.

Acknowledging the possibility of danger in a situation does not necessarily make you an anxious person. You may be a realist. But if your focus is constantly on the possible harm, or on the one factor that could go wrong, or whether you did the right thing, you are an anxious thinker. Anxious thinking makes anxious people, but by changing your thoughts, you can lessen your anxiety and even the feelings that result from those thoughts.

CONTAIN STRESSFUL THOUGHTS

Stress can originate from your thoughts. Two good strategies to help with stressful thoughts are visualizing and meditation. We are not talking about repeating mantras or engaging in transcendental meditation, so please stay with us. Christians can meditate and visualize. The Bible even directs us to do so: "Whatever is true, whatever is noble, whatever is right, whatever is pure, whatever is lovely, whatever is admirable—if anything is excellent or praiseworthy—think about such things" (Philippians 4:8 NIV).

All we do is focus our minds on what brings us peace and a sense of wellbeing. We need to just think about God's intense love for us and dedicate some time to Him. When we pray and spend time with our heavenly Father, we feel better and less stressed. This Dad has promised to take care of us and meet our needs. If that reality doesn't lessen our stress, nothing will!

True peace comes from having a personal relationship with Jesus Christ. One of His promises is to keep us in perfect peace if we keep our minds fixed on Him (Isaiah 26:3). God is the author of peace and serenity. We need to think about Him and His goodness, love, and all that He has done for us and will do as we approach His eternal presence.

A renewed mind is a mind that agrees with God. God is incapable of having bad motivations toward us, and yet we often attribute these to God. In Him, there is no darkness. When we know His character, His promises, and we believe who He says He is, we cannot think of God as bad or unloving. The key is intimacy with Him. The more we know Him, the more we trust and believe that He is truth. And the more time we spend with Him, the more we experience His truth.

In 2 Corinthians 1:8–9, Paul affirms that God brings comfort in the midst of trouble: "We don't want you in the dark, friends, about how hard it was when all this came down on us in Asia province. It was so bad we didn't think we were going to make it. We felt like we'd been sent to death row, that it was all over for us. As it turned out, it was the best thing that could have happened. Instead of trusting in our own strength or wits to get out of it, we were forced to trust God totally—not a bad idea since he's the God who raises the dead!" (MSG).

Sometimes we think too much! It is easy to question God in times of difficulty. We can grow impatient and allow the enemy to gain ground in our thoughts. But God wants to teach us to depend on Him all the time as we renew our minds with His truth and know that He is powerful and able to accomplish much in us if we submit to His plan.

Cast your burden on the LORD,
And He shall sustain you;
He shall never permit the righteous to be moved.

Psalm 55:22

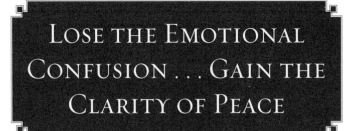

LOSE THE EMOTIONAL CONFUSION . . . GAIN THE CLARITY OF PEACE

Is anyone among you suffering? Let him pray.
Is anyone cheerful? Let him sing psalms.

James 5:13

Our emotions are very much part of who we are and how we perceive the world, but all too often we give our emotions too much control in our lives. We need to get better understanding of them, so we can manage them in better accordance with God's will. Here are some of the main emotional states that trouble us.

ANGER

Anger feels uncomfortable and is often confused with a need to eat or to act out in some other self–indulgent manner. The biblical directive given in Ephesians 4:26 is, "Be angry, and do not sin." This scripture affirms anger as part of our human nature but also tells us not to sin in response to that emotion. Yet anger will not go away on its own. To be rid of it requires recognizing anger, acknowledging you have it, and then dealing with it according to these biblical guidelines:

James 1:19—*Be quick to listen, slow to speak and slow to become angry* (NIV).

Proverbs 29:11— *Foolish people lose their tempers, but wise people control theirs* (NCV).

Proverbs 15:1—*A gentle answer will calm a person's anger, but an unkind answer will cause more anger* (NCV).

Matthew 6:14—*If you forgive others for their sins, your Father in heaven will also forgive you for your sins* (NCV).

Psalm 4:4—*Be angry, and do not sin. Meditate within your heart on your bed, and be still* (NKJV).

1 Peter 5:7—*Give all your worries to him, because he cares about you* (NCV).

Proverbs 22:24—*Don't make friends with quick-tempered people or spend time with those who have bad tempers* (NCV).

FATIGUE

If you are tired, rest is what you need for both your body and your spirit. Food or caffeine may give you a temporary surge, but you will end up feeling more sluggish and still tired in the long run. Rest, exercise, and eat well. Rest is biblical—even God rested after creating the world.

Psalm 37:7—*Rest in the LORD and wait patiently for Him* (NKJV).

Matthew 11:28–30—*"Are you tired? Worn out? Burned out on religion? Come to me. Get away with me and you'll recover your life. I'll show you how to take a real rest. Walk with me and work with me—watch how I do it. Learn the unforced rhythms of grace. I won't lay anything heavy or ill-fitting on you. Keep company with me and you'll learn to live freely and lightly"* (MSG).

Hebrews 4:1—*For as long, then, as that promise of resting in him pulls us on to God's goal for us, we need to be careful that we're not disqualified* (MSG).

Hebrews 4:9—*The promise of "arrival" and "rest" is still there for God's people* (MSG).

DEPRESSION

Your most powerful weapon against depression is praise. We are told in Isaiah 61:3 to put on a garment of praise for a spirit of despair. Don't wait to feel like you want to praise. Do it no matter what you feel like. Praise God for who He is. Praise is the antidote to feeling down. Let His praise be in your mouth continuously (Psalm 34:1), and the Lord will lift your spirit.

If you struggle with clinical depression, there is nothing wrong with going on an antidepressant to help stabilize your moods and correct your brain chemistry. Taking medication does not demonstrate a lack of faith. Antidepressants are simply agents used to get you living well again by restoring proper brain functioning. All healing comes through God, but He uses both miracles and medicine to accomplish His purposes. You may need to see a doctor and/or a therapist to help with depression.

TRANSFORMATION

LONELINESS

When you are lonely, you may overindulge in food or television or some other solitary, always–available pursuit instead of engaging in activities that could end your loneliness. Therefore you must find other ways to deal with loneliness. Join an organization, volunteer your time, enroll in a class, become active with a charity, attend a church function, or make the first move and call someone you'd like to befriend. Also, listen carefully for what God may be trying to teach you or ask of you, because many of His greatest servants have experienced great loneliness (1 Kings 19:3–14; Jeremiah 15:17; Nehemiah 2:12–16; Matthew 26:36–45).

INADEQUACY

You are inadequate because you are human. You must learn to accept your weaknesses and flaws and not dwell on them. And when you feel inadequate or weak, it helps to know that God is strong and can work through you anyway.

Make a list of your strengths and weaknesses. Try to focus on those things you do well. Then ask God to help you with your weaknesses. By His Spirit, He is able to accomplish much, even with your limitations (Zechariah 4:6).

TRANSFORMATION

This is an area that has plagued me since I was a child. My first problem was an obsession with others and comparing myself to them, trying to figure out where I was on the food chain. I wanted so much and to do so much while always feeling I had too little. It wasn't until I finally realized that the curse of not being as talented or having as much as others was actually a gift. The gift was knowing that God had done things through me in spite of my inadequacies rather than because of my strengths. It was a gift to see that although I did not measure up, God used me to become part of His kingdom–building project.

If you start to look at your emotions and find that inadequacy is at the top of the list, give up on trying to feel better about yourself and start focusing on feeling better about God. Look at what God has done through you. Look at what God has allowed to happen in your life even though you did not have it all together or have all that others had.

INSECURITY

The only place you are truly secure is in your relationship with God. A multitude of scriptures speak to who we are in

Christ—we are loved, forgiven, saved by grace through faith, joint heirs with Christ, blessed with all spiritual blessings, sons and daughters of God, complete in Him, and so much more. It may help you to do a study on scriptures related to our security in Christ. Here are a few to get you started:

Psalm 34:4—*I asked the LORD for help, and he answered me. He saved me from all that I feared* (NCV).

Deuteronomy 31:8—*"The LORD himself will go before you. He will be with you; he will not leave you or forget you. Don't be afraid and don't worry"* (NCV).

Romans 8:28—*We know that all things work together for good to those who love God, to those who are the called according to His purpose* (NKJV).

2 Corinthians 1:21–22—*God is the One who makes you and us strong in Christ. God made us his chosen people. He put his mark on us to show that we are his, and he put his Spirit in our hearts to be a guarantee for all he has promised* (NCV).

GUILT

Guilt is only healthy when it relates to sin. You should feel guilty when you go against God's Word and sin. But once you confess that sin, it is gone and forgotten. To hang on to guilt serves no good purpose. Jesus does not accuse (John 5:45) nor condemn you (Romans 8:1). When you own your mistakes and take responsibility for them, you must let go of condemnation and unhealthy guilt—to not do so is to ignore the power of the blood covenant over past sins. You may intellectually know that Jesus died on the cross to take your sins, yet be unable to get past your mistakes. So you walk around carrying tremendous guilt and shame, yet Christ died so you could give Him these sins and burdens. Hand them over and walk with your head held high.

The apostle Paul explained what God is really after when believers do something wrong: "Now I am happy, not because you were made sad, but because your sorrow made you change your lives. You became sad in the way God wanted you to. . . . The kind of sorrow God wants makes people change their hearts and lives. This leads to salvation, and you cannot be sorry for that. But the kind of sorrow the world has brings death" (2 Corinthians 7:9–10 NCV). Godly sorrow will move you to change. It will motivate you toward God and relationship with Him. So feel the guilt, confess it, and then turn it into a spiritual experience of godly sorrow that increases your character.

SHAME

Shame comes when you've done something improper or wrong and you internalize "badness" because of it. Shame says, "I am a mistake," not "I made a mistake." Shame often develops from a message that you are bad, weak, or unloved.

If you are feeling shame right now, you need to embrace that shame and allow yourself to feel it. Understand, it's going to feel awful, but don't push it away or try to avoid it. Then ask the Lord to show you the source of that pain—a cruel word, a disappointing look, a moment of rejection. Let your mind go wherever the Holy Spirit takes you.

With that memory in mind, try to think why you feel shame. What thought comes to your mind? Is it *I am a bad person* or *I don't deserve to be treated nicely*? Be honest with what you are thinking. The thought is most likely a lie. Once you've identified the lie, ask Jesus to speak His truth to you. Wait and allow Him to speak truth. What do you see or hear Him say? His truth will set you free from that shame. Then, forgive the person who did or said something that created that feeling of shame.

Shame is a deep internal response of feeling unworthy in another person's eyes. It can be experienced through unkind words and actions. But understand something important. Jesus does not shame you. He sees you as worthy and valuable! When He sees the shame you experience, He urges you to bring it to the cross. He died for it.

The life lived with God is a great adventure, much like a rollercoaster ride. It is filled with ups and downs to be experienced. When you experience the downside, find your worth in Him and hand over the shame. He's with you on the journey.

JEALOUSY

Just because others are thin or well-dressed doesn't mean they are happy and living a good life. Jesus tells us to "Stop judging by the way things look, but judge by what is really right" (John 7:24 NCV). He is not impressed with people who seem to be important. And Paul followed Christ by saying, "As for those who seemed to be important—whatever they were makes no difference to me; God does not judge by external appearance—those men added nothing to my message" (Galatians 2:6 NIV). So stop comparing yourself to others. Jealousy is a very unproductive emotion.

TRANSFORMATION

HAPPINESS

Recognize that while happiness comes and goes, you always have joy in the Lord; joy is your strength.

Psalm 19:8—*The precepts of the* LORD *are right, giving joy to the heart. The commands of the* LORD *are radiant, giving light to the eyes* (NIV).

James 5:13—*Is anyone among you suffering? Let him pray. Is anyone cheerful? Let him sing psalms* (NKJV).

Acts 14:17—*"He proved he is real by showing kindness, by giving you rain from heaven and crops at the right times, by giving you food and filling your hearts with joy"* (NCV).

Psalm 28:7—*The* LORD *is my strength and my shield; my heart trusted in Him, and I am helped. Therefore my heart greatly rejoices, and with my song I will praise Him* (NKJV).

ANXIETY, WORRY, AND FEAR

In today's world, there are endless situations over which to worry. Psalm 139:23–24 says, "Search me, O God, and know my heart; try me, and know my anxieties; and see if there is any

wicked way in me, and lead me in the way everlasting" (NKJV).
God knows if we are anxious! He wants us to stop feeling
responsible and worried for those things we can't control. Jesus
tells us not to worry even about our basic needs in life (Matthew
6:25–34).

Worry paralyzes our faith and draws our attention away from
the faithfulness of God. Paul tells us to be anxious about nothing
(Philippians 4:6) and then explains how we can accomplish this—
by thanking God and sharing our concerns with Him through
prayer. That is to be followed by meditating on God's goodness.
The result is His supernatural peace resting on us.

Numerous times in the Bible we are told to fast against fear.

1 John 4:18—*Where God's love is, there is no fear, because God's perfect love drives
out fear. It is punishment that makes a person fear, so love is not made perfect in the person
who fears* (NCV).

Isaiah 35:4—*Tell fearful souls, "Courage! Take heart! GOD is here, right here,
on his way to put things right and redress all wrongs. He's on his way! He'll save you!"*
(MSG).

DISAPPOINTMENT AND HURT

There are so many opportunities to be disappointed with others that we could spend our whole lives drowning in this one emotion. People make mistakes, betray us, act in self–centered ways, and fail to look out for our best interests. Thus, our faith and confidence must be in the Lord instead, and even then, we may feel letdown or hurt.

If this is the case, there is a problem of trust in God. He orders your steps and will allow difficulty in your life for a purpose (James 1:2–4). However, God's promise is to be with you through tough times. Focus on what you can learn from disappointment, but trust God to work it for your own good in His due time and in His way.

Isaiah 26:3–4—*You will keep in perfect peace him whose mind is steadfast, because he trusts in you. Trust in the LORD forever, for the LORD, the LORD, is the Rock eternal* (NIV).

EMPTINESS

So many people go through life feeling empty and without purpose. Nothing will fill that void like an authentic relationship with God. He desires to draw close and be with you. He wants to fill you with good things and has a plan and purpose for you specifically. Engage with God in a new way. Be filled with His Word, and when you feel empty, hunger and thirst for righteousness so that you will be filled (Matthew 5:6). Only God can come close to fulfilling us. Emptiness leads us to fill our lives with everything but the one thing we truly need—God.

REJECTION

Rejection is hard to handle under any circumstances, but it is especially difficult to swallow when it comes from those who are supposed to love you. To be healed, you must face rejection. Feel it with all your soul. Pour out your heart to the Lord. Once you've allowed yourself to really feel the pain of rejection, pray and ask God to take it. Then ask Christ to speak His truth to you. You see, the enemy used emotional pain to implant lies—that no one will want or love you; that people will only hurt you; that if only you were better . . . all lies!

TRANSFORMATION

The truth is that there is someone who is completely trustworthy and who will never reject you. Your acceptance has nothing to do with your actions or your appearance. Jesus unconditionally loves you because you are His. He identifies with your pain. According to Isaiah 53, Christ was despised, rejected, and a man of sorrow. Because of His great love for you, He suffered the pain of rejection and crucified it once and for all on the cross. Once you allow His truth to soak into your spirit, you can give up the pain of rejection and accept God's unfailing love.

If you've suffered a number of rejections, try to understand that those people were probably not rejecting you personally as much as the concept of you or what you represented. If you suffered parental rejection, for example, your parents probably rejected the concept of having to meet someone else's needs, rather than rejecting you as an individual. Rejection still hurts, but it may be easier to forgive someone once you realize that person had problems of his/her own that were taken out on you. Whatever the case, you will need to forgive those who rejected you.

LOSS OF CONTROL

Control is elusive. You are not in control, so you might as well surrender to the One who is.

TRANSFORMATION

EXPRESS YOUR FEELINGS

Once you have identified your feelings, you must learn to express them directly rather than medicating them with food, entertainment, work, or other temporary solutions. Feelings can be expressed by talking them out to a friend, writing them in a journal, and/or by crying and giving direct vent to feelings. For example, you might say aloud, "I am so sad right now because I feel ignored." Give verbal expression to your feelings instead of swallowing them or stuffing them away. Allow yourself to feel whatever the feeling is until the intensity subsides. Then determine if there is a need behind the feeling, such as a need to be loved, accepted, approved, or respected. Get to the heart of the feeling and decide if you are being realistic. If you must grieve a loss or work on ways to get your needs met, deal with the feelings.

You now have sorrow; but I will see you again and your heart will rejoice, and your joy no one will take from you.

John 16:22

TRANSFORMATION

LOSE THE STRESS . . . GAIN A RELAXED SPIRIT

Rest in the LORD, and wait patiently for Him;
Do not fret because of him who prospers in his way,
Because of the man who brings wicked schemes to pass.
Cease from anger, and forsake wrath;
Do not fret—it only causes harm.

Psalm 37:7–8

You'd have to be living on another planet not to know that stress affects your body in negative ways. Because stress is something we all experience, we all need to learn effective ways to manage or reduce it. Begin to evaluate what you are doing that may add stress to your life. Are there habits and practices you could change today that would make you feel better? The answer is probably yes. Think about your response to stress in terms of self–care. How will you take care of yourself in order to battle the negative effects of stress?

TRANSFORMATION

1. Do you have effective ways of relaxing? We all need downtime. Relaxation isn't something you just do once a year on a cruise to the Bahamas (although this certainly can help). Relaxing should be a regular, practiced part of your life. You need balance in all things. Even God rested on the seventh day (Genesis 2:2–3)! Relaxation keeps stress from building up and provides an avenue for releasing tension.

2. Do you regularly exercise? The benefits of exercise are enormous. Exercise can reduce muscle tension and frustration in addition to providing a host of medical helps. Find something you enjoy—bike riding, dancing, skating, basketball, tennis, skiing, walking—anything that gets you off that couch and moving.

3. How sensibly do you eat? Do you eat good food that provides nutrition and health benefits? Do you skip meals? Eat burgers in the car while talking on the cell phone? Find yourself at the drive–through regularly?

4. How well do you manage your time? So many people spend energy on things that are unproductive or take up too much of their time. If you are missing deadlines or procrastinating or obsessing over projects, you need help. Some people have to learn to move along more efficiently, while others need to slow down and do things correctly. Because your time is limited, it's important to learn to prioritize and be realistic about goals.

5. Are you getting enough sleep? This sounds like a simple question, but so many people have terrible sleep habits. Going to bed at a regular time and getting into a sleep routine is essential. A lack of sleep is associated with changes in hormone levels. When cortisol levels remain high from a lack of sleep, the body craves carbohydrates and foods high in calories and fat. Metabolism then slows down as the body stores fat. And here's an encouraging thought for those to whom it morally applies—sex usually helps people sleep. Now there's a sleep motivator we can live with!

Now godliness with contentment is great gain.
For we brought nothing into this world,
and it is certain we can carry nothing out.
And having food and clothing, with these we shall be content.

1 *Timothy 6:6–8*

LOSE THE ANTI-EXERCISE ATTITUDE . . . GAIN A LIVELIER LIFE

God is my strength and power,
And He makes my way perfect.
He makes my feet like the feet of deer,
And sets me on my high places.

2 Samuel 22:33–34

L ike it or not, we all need to exercise if we want to live to enjoy the blessings of life and opportunities of service God has ordained for us. Exercise has numerous benefits. Here are six of the main ones:

1. Exercise helps reduce hidden belly fat, lowering the risk of heart disease, diabetes, stroke, and some types of cancer.

2. Exercise prevents muscle from wasting and helps to lose fat.

3. Exercise helps the brain deal with stress more effectively.

4. Moderate cardiovascular exercise such as thirty minutes of brisk walking a few times a week can improve your memory.

5. Exercise helps manage hunger. Research shows that exercising increases control over hunger and food intake. In fact, the physically fit person is often not hungry until several hours after exercise.

6. Exercise improves your immune system.

When it comes to making exercise a habit, attitude is more than half the battle. Whatever reasons you have used for avoiding exercise in the past—it's unpleasant, too painful, inconvenient, frustrating, or too time consuming—the reality is that exercise is necessary if you are serious about being healthy. Regardless of your past experiences, regular physical activity is essential for developing a healthy lifestyle.

One way to succeed in an exercise program is to match exercise with who you are. Choose activities that mesh well with who you are and what you like to do, and you'll be more likely to stick to them. And if an activity provides mental relaxation and enjoyment, you'll receive double the benefits!

Consistent exercise will take commitment, but you can do this with God's help and with the help of others. Success is at the end of many tasks like healthy eating, getting enough sleep, and spending time with the Lord each day. Boundaries and accountability are necessary.

You take care of yourself by setting boundaries with your time and energy so that there is time for the priorities such as healthy eating and exercising. Decide that the times you designate for fitness, nutrition, spiritual focus, and personal growth are nonnegotiable. This means exercising should not be the first thing you take out of your schedule if life's "stuff" gets in the way. Make every effort to stick with your routine. There is grace for those times when you let life crowd out your personal commitments, but you must make it a priority to get back on track and make time for exercise.

If you do not carve out time for your physical, spiritual, and personal needs, you will burn out, bum out, and bail out by acting out. Overeating, overworking, increased drinking, anger, depression, worry, and anxiety are all symptoms of burnout. Create good habits and routines for exercise, nutrition, and

TRANSFORMATION

spiritual and personal time so you won't burn out.

It's best to set short– and long–term goals for your exercise routine. If you have difficulty exercising, a good short–term goal may be to walk for five minutes at least two days per week for two weeks. A long–term goal may be to walk forty minutes most days of the week after nine months. Writing down your progress in a journal is an excellent way to track goals and stay on track. Though you may not feel like you are making progress within a given week, when you look back at where you started, you may be pleasantly surprised!

Also, support is a key factor in staying motivated. An exercise buddy can cheer you on and hold you accountable. For women in particular, it's a good way to feel safe while exercising outdoors.

The goal is to find whatever is necessary—tools, books, therapists, or personal trainers—to help you establish a routine you can do for the rest of your life. If you approach a routine with this mindset, finding a pace that is workable will be easier and you will be more likely to stick with it.

Please don't allow negative past experiences to stop you from doing what is in your heart to do. You can be victorious in this journey. God knows your physical and emotional pain and isn't judging you, and there are people who can and will support you in this endeavor.

As you begin to exercise, you may encounter people who don't understand and who may judge you. Yet God sees and knows what you are going through. As Paul admonished, "Forgetting those things which are behind, [we] press toward the goal" (Philippians 3:13–14). Don't focus on what you can't do or how others may perceive you. Instead, reflect on each small step you make and recognize those steps for what they are—individual acts of courage.

Exercise isn't an option if you want to reap the benefits of a healthy life; it's a necessity. Whatever your pleasure, there is an activity that is right for you, but it's up to you to find that exercise and get moving. Whether it's walking, aerobics, weightlifting, stretching, or even taking the stairs instead of the elevator, each small change will make a difference in your health, weight maintenance, and mental health. So get motivated and get moving!

Beloved, I pray that you may prosper in all things and be in health, just as your soul prospers. For I rejoiced greatly when brethren came and testified of the truth that is in you, just as you walk in the truth. I have no greater joy than to hear that my children walk in truth.

3 John 2–4

TRANSFORMATION

FIVE KEYS TO SUCCESS IN YOUR EXERCISE PROGRAM

1. Make exercise convenient. Try to fit it into your lunch hour or even while you're watching TV. Just get started and remind yourself of what you hope to gain.

2. Make it fun. There is nothing worse than being bored or hating what you're doing. Find something you enjoy.

3. Enjoy variety. Mix it up. You don't have to walk every day! You can take a bike ride one day, walk the next, and skate in the park the third day. Make sure you do a variety of aerobic, stretching, and strength–training exercises.

4. Add music to the routine. Listening to music may make exercising more enjoyable, and it often adds extra motivation to a workout.

5. Exercise with a partner or friend. A partner can provide accountability and encouragement. When you commit to someone else, you have added motivation to make the time and fulfill your commitment, but you also add fun! If you prefer a solo workout, that's fine too. Just decide what works best for you and get moving.

LOSE THE LONELINESS OF ISOLATION . . . GAIN THE POWER OF CONNECTION

Two people are better than one,
because they get more done by working together.
If one falls down,
the other can help him up.
But it is bad for the person who is alone and falls,
because no one is there to help.
If two lie down together, they will be warm,
but a person alone will not be warm.
An enemy might defeat one person,
but two people together can defend themselves;
a rope that is woven of three strings is hard to break.

Ecclesiastes 4:9–12 NCV

R elationship has existed since before time began. Relationship started with the Godhead—they are three in one, a Trinity that enjoys fellowship. Then at the dawn of creation, God created woman because it was not good for man to be alone (Genesis 2:18). A central message of Jesus' teaching was for us to live in unity with one another (John 17:20–23), and when Jesus returned to the Father, the Holy Spirit was sent as Comforter (Acts 9:31). Clearly, relationship is essential to who we are.

We need each other. As we encourage one another and uplift each other in prayer, we move forward in the Christian life in ways not possible as loners. Relationships are important for meeting our needs for intimacy and support, but also for growing and avoiding relapse into old habits. In order to RISE above the challenges, we need connection and community.

Reduce negative relationships that sabotage the positive changes we want to make in our lives.

Increase our connection with others, our social skills, and the sizes of our communities.

Substitute the healing of community and connection for the belief that we must go it alone.

Eliminate the lone ranger mentality and toxic relationships that undermine our success.

YOU NEED THE BODY

It helps to remember the source of your true worth. Jesus Christ says you are already accepted, loved, and special (John 6:37; 16:27). Other people may not always be so positive and affirming. However, some people will be, and you must find them and make a connection. You need their support and encouragement.

One reason people struggle even when they know how important their relationship with Christ is to succeeding in any endeavor of life is because they are not connected to a community of fellow believers. No matter how successful you are at striving for your goals, you need connections with people who can help when you feel down or want to give in and give up.

When you are the consummate giver and never expect to receive in a relationship, you tend to attract needy people who can suck you dry. And then, guess what? You feel empty. However, in the body of Christ, when you feel strong, you encourage another, and when you are down, another person encourages you. This give–and–take is the basis for healthy relationships.

REVIST SOCIAL SKILLS

When you begin to take risks socially, you must also take a hard look at your social skills. Maybe you need to be more assertive, learn how to initiate conversation, or demonstrate a new interest in others. Personal improvements such as a new look or a special accomplishment may boost your confidence, but it won't teach you social skills. You may have to practice some new ones.

DON'T ALIENATE YOURSELF

Shame, fear, embarrassment, or even thinking we lack good social skills are reasons that keep many of us away from the very people whose support we need. Another significant isolating factor is pride. We convince ourselves that needing others is too painful or is weakness. We think we really don't need people to help us in life because we've bought into the independence–minded idealism of doing it on our own. We try to gut it out, and we believe our failure to succeed is because we lack willpower, not because we need others along the way.

In some cases our lack of experience with healthy relationships keeps us from trying. Growing up alone and isolated, we see no benefit in relationships. Our experiences only brought hurt. Or in cases where relationships may have started out strong, we were betrayed or disappointed. We believe people cannot be trusted or that we will be rejected.

Many of us give up on relationships and fail to distinguish between the benefits of healthy relationships and the needy and overly dependent relationships in which we may be entwined. The former are healthy; the latter are toxic.

Yet, even with all our reasons for pulling back and protecting ourselves from hurt or pain, we still desire connection. We were created to relate to God and others. It is in relationships that we grow and learn about ourselves. Through our experiences with others, we define how we think and feel. Attachment is a basic need that never goes away but longs to be met.

The need for connection is not unhealthy, but how we meet that need can be. In God's kingdom, nobody is more important than the next (1 Corinthians 12:15–19). We approach each other with humility and must have the courage to be open to what we can receive from others. Yes, we can be rejected, but we also can find people who will accept and love us no matter what we weigh or how many times we fail. If we don't allow bad relationships to derail our efforts, we can have meaningful connections and our needs will be met.

Healthy relationships include loving God, ourselves, and others. We don't love with a puffed-up sense of importance (1 Corinthians 13:4). We love because God loves us and has purpose and meaning for our lives (Ephesians 1:5). As we surrender to that purpose and plan, we purposefully connect with others to accomplish what we can't accomplish alone. Connection brings healing and healing brings joy.

When we are willing to be open, transparent, and vulnerable to others, we break free of the isolation that keeps us hidden in the dark. We feel God's love because we aren't moving in pretense. We learn to accept who we are because we are in process. We ask for healing so we can grow and give to others and find rest.

To move out of the victim position would mean forgiving people and making other changes. Giving up anything you know well to move into the unknown is always a bit unsettling, but the gains are certainly worth a bit of anxiety. A lack of trust is at the root of this problem. You must trust that being obedient to God's Word, as well as forgiving others' wrongs and extending grace, will turn out beneficial to you and others in the long run. Don't allow bitterness to prevent you from moving forward.

If you decide to be more vulnerable and open your life up to others, recognize that it won't be easy or a positive experience 100 percent of the time. You'll have times of frustration, and you'll learn who can handle your openness and who cannot. Some people simply are not trustworthy, and you must be discerning about opening up to the right people. Yet be careful how you do this! Paul addressed how we are to behave with one another in Romans 14:1–9:

> *Welcome with open arms fellow believers who don't see things the way you do. And don't jump all over them every time they do or say something you don't agree with—even when it seems that they are strong on opinions but weak in the faith department. Remember, they have their own history to deal with. Treat them gently.*

> *For instance, a person who has been around for a while might well be convinced that he can eat anything on the table, while another, with a different background, might assume he should only be a vegetarian and eat accordingly. But since both are guests at Christ's table, wouldn't it be terribly rude if they fell to criticizing what the other ate or didn't eat? God, after all, invited them both to the table. Do you have any business crossing people*

*off the guest list or interfering with God's welcome? If there are
corrections to be made or manners to be learned, God can handle
that without your help.*

*Or, say, one person thinks that some days should be set aside as
holy and another thinks that each day is pretty much like any
other. There are good reasons either way. So, each person is free
to follow the convictions of conscience.*

*What's important in all this is that if you keep a holy day, keep it for
God's sake; if you eat meat, eat it to the glory of God and thank God
for prime rib; if you're a vegetarian, eat vegetables to the glory of God
and thank God for broccoli. None of us are permitted to insist on our
own way in these matters. It's God we are answerable to—all the way
from life to death and everything in between—not each other. That's
why Jesus lived and died and then lived again: so that he could be our
Master across the entire range of life and death, and free us from the
petty tyrannies of each other* (MSG).

If we allow Jesus to be our Master who can "free us from the
petty tyrannies of each other," dynamic things will happen. We
all have differences that can divide us if we let them. However,
we are called to unity and we should work out our differences in
Christian love and maturity. The resulting unity will create an

atmosphere for healing. Make it your goal to find people with whom you can be authentic, who will maintain confidences and pray with you. Work on your differences with others and learn to live in Christian love.

Relationships are work because they often act as mirrors to our own problems. In intimacy, we see our weaknesses and need for God's help. As we grow, we become aware of our separateness, but also our need for each other. As we learn to define who we are, set boundaries, deal with conflict, and manage differences, we grow if we stay connected to others in the process.

What should we look for when it comes to building relationships with one another? Ephesians 4:2 says, "Always be humble, gentle, and patient, accepting each other in love" (NCV). We are to pursue community with one another and be patient and humble in the process.

Jesus recognized the need for community in His darkest hour. He took His disciples with Him to pray as He faced the biggest challenge of His earthly life—the cross. As He hung on the cross, He thought of others and even welcomed a thief into Paradise! He also arranged for John, the beloved, to care for His mother. And in those last moments before His death, He cried out from a sense of estrangement, "My God, my God, why have you forsaken me?" (Matthew 27:46). For a brief moment, He felt abandoned by the Father and became a curse for us (Galatians 3:13).

Jesus is all about community. He says that people will know His followers by their love (John 13:35) and that believers are to love one another. When you face any difficult change or trial in your life, support and community make the difference in your ability to survive and come through the trial. Seek wise counsel from those who can help you. Be responsive to your pastors and leaders who will provide spiritual accountability. Take advantage of counselors and therapists who can help you sort out the complexity of your specific problems. Be persistent and have the courage to be open in relationships with others.

***

All praise to the God and Father of our Master, Jesus
the Messiah! Father of all mercy! God of all healing counsel!
He comes alongside us when we go through hard times,
and before you know it, he brings us alongside someone else who is
going through hard times so that we can be there for that person
just as God was there for us.

2 Corinthians 1:3–4 (MSG)

***

PRESERVATION

What a fabulous verse! God comes alongside of us when we go through difficulty. That in and of itself is reassuring, but there is even more—God will use us to help someone else who is going through a hard time as well. In God's economy, nothing is ever wasted, not even pain!

We can never know God's plans or His gain from our loss unless we give Him our misery and allow Him to transform it into a mission for our lives. Once our loss and pain point us to God's grace, we can also lead others into His grace. In doing so, we partner with God as He accomplishes His purposes. After we emerge from our own despair, become transparent, and candidly share our victories, we will be in a position to share our struggles and God's power to overcome, attracting others into His grace.

God's church is our earthly home. Embrace the love and support He has instituted for you and build on that connection for life.

PRESERVATION

We pray that you will also have great wisdom and understanding in spiritual things so that you will live the kind of life that honors and pleases the Lord in every way. You will produce fruit in every good work and grow in the knowledge of God. God will strengthen you with his own great power so that you will not give up when troubles come, but you will be patient. And you will joyfully give thanks to the Father who has made you able to have a share in all that he has prepared for his people in the kingdom of light. God has freed us from the power of darkness, and he brought us into the kingdom of his dear Son.

Colossians 1:9–13 NCV

PRESERVATION

❧❀❧

The LORD upholds all who fall,

And raises up all who are bowed down.

The eyes of all look expectantly to You,

And You give them their food in due season.

You open Your hand

And satisfy the desire of every living thing.

The LORD is righteous in all His ways,

Gracious in all His works.

The LORD is near to all who call upon Him,

To all who call upon Him in truth.

He will fulfill the desire of those who fear Him;

He also will hear their cry and save them.

The LORD preserves all who love Him,

But all the wicked He will destroy.

My mouth shall speak the praise of the LORD,

And all flesh shall bless His holy name

Forever and ever.

Psalm 145:14–21

❧❀❧

CONCLUSION

So, now that you've basically finished this book, have you made all the changes you need to make in your life? Have you lost everything you needed to lose and gained all you desire? Of course not! Not yet. Change takes time. But the fact that you've persisted in reading the previous 126 pages of this book demonstrates your commitment to the process. Keep going! You can do this!

What have you got to lose?

An unsatisfying way of life.

What have you got to gain?

All that God longs to give you.

Go for it!

FOR MORE INFORMATION

If the information in this book has been helpful to you, you might want to explore these concepts as they apply specifically to weight loss. Read *Lose It For Life: The Total Solution—Spiritual, Emotional, Physical—for Permanent Weight Loss*, by Stephen Arterburn and Linda Mintle (Integrity, 2004).

For additional perspectives on the "7 Keys," read Stephen Arterburn's book *Transformation: Turn Your Life Around Starting Today*, co-written with David Stoop (Tyndale, 2006).

For more insights on "The Godly Tools for Action," read *Soul on Fire: Discover Your Life's Passion and Purpose* (Tyndale, 2006).

To learn more about other life-changing resources, please visit www.newlife.com or call 1-800-NEW-LIFE.